Traverse Theatre Company

ARCTIC OIL
by Clare Duffy

Commissioned by the Traverse Theatre and the Institute for Advanced Studies in the Humanities (IASH), University of Edinburgh, and first performed at the Traverse Theatre, Scotland, on 9 October 2018.

COMPANY LIST

Cast

Mother	Jennifer Black
Daughter	Neshla Caplan

Creative Team

Writer	Clare Duffy
Director	Gareth Nicholls
Lighting Designer	Renny Robertson
Composer & Sound Designer	Stephen Jones
Costume Designer	Sophie Ferguson
Fight Director	Raymond Short
Set Design	Gareth Nicholls & Kevin McCallum

Production Team

Production Manager	Kevin McCallum
Chief Electrician	Renny Robertson
Deputy Electrician	Claire Elliot
Head of Stage	Gary Staerck
Lighting & Sound Technician	Tom Saunders
Company Stage Manager	Gemma Turner
Deputy Stage Manager	Naomi Stalker

COMPANY BIOGRAPHIES

Jennifer Black (Mother)

Recent theatre credits include: *The Iliad, Tartuffe, Six Black Candles, A Streetcar Named Desire, Peter Pan, Macbeth, An Experienced Woman Gives Advice, Dead Funny, On Golden Pond, Blithe Spirit* (Royal Lyceum Theatre Edinburgh); *The Cone Gatherers* (Aberdeen Performing Arts); *Safe Place, 10,000 Metres Deep, Leather Bound* (Òran Mór); *A Taste of Honey* (TAG Theatre); *Three Thousand Troubled Threads, The Memory of Water* (Stellar Quines); *Thebans* (Theatre Babel); *Falling, Buried Treasure* (Bush Theatre); *Too Late for Logic* (King's Theatre); *One Good Beating, Kill the Old Torture their Young, House Among the Stars, The Bench* (Traverse Theatre); *Stiff The Musical* (Diva Productions); *Lavochkin-5, Ashes to Ashes, The Trick is to Keep Breathing, Good, The Baby* (Tron Theatre); *Sacred Hearts* (Communicado).

Jennifer's film and television credits include: *Shetland, Doctors, Holby City, Half Moon Investigations, Still Game, River City, Why Do They Call It Good Friday, A View of Things, The Ploughman's Lunch* (BBC); *Rebus* (SMG); *Tinsel Town, Taggart, Out in the Open, Ugly Sisters* (STV); *I Saw You* (Channel 4); *The Bill* (Thames Television); *Local Hero* (Goldcrest Films); *Heavenly Pursuits* (Skebo Films).

Jennifer's radio credits include: *Under the Skin, Week Ending, The Trick is to Keep Breathing* (BBC Radio 4).

Neshla Caplan (Daughter)

Neshla trained at the Royal Conservatoire of Scotland.

Recent theatre credits: *Sunshine on Leith* (West Yorkshire Playhouse); *Arabian Nights, The BFG* (Royal Lyceum Theatre Edinburgh); *The Sunshine Ghost* (Scottish Theatre Producers/ Festival & King's Theatres, Edinburgh); *Adam* (National Theatre of Scotland); *Breakfast Plays: Youthquake* (Traverse Theatre); *WEE FREE! The Musical, Voices in Her Ear* (Òran Mór); *The Progressive Playwright* (Tron Theatre); *The Choir* (Citizens Theatre/Ambassador Theatre Group); *The Girl Who* (Noisemaker/Theatre Bench/ Royal Conservatoire of Scotland); *The Addams Family* (Royal Conservatoire of Scotland).

Clare Duffy (Writer)

Clare is a playwright and director. She is the Artistic Director of Civic Digits and Co-Director of Unlimited Theatre, which she co-founded in 1997.

In August 2018, Clare presented a musical scratch performance of *How to Be Both* by Ali Smith at the Edinburgh International Book Festival in association with the Royal Lyceum Theatre Edinburgh.

She is an associate artist at Perth Theatre, making *The Big Data Show*, which integrates ethical hacking, digital gaming and live performance. She recently co-wrote *Future Bodies* with Abbi Greenland, a co-production between RashDash, Unlimited Theatre and Home, Manchester. She was dramaturg for *The Reason I Jump* by Naoki Higashida, produced by the National Theatre of Scotland in May 2018, and directed by Graham Eatough.

Clare has written the CBeebies' Christmas show since 2013, and adapted *A Midsummer Night's Dream* for CBeebies in 2016, which won the Royal Television Society's Award for Best Children's Programme.

She wrote and directed *Money: The Game Show* for The Arches in 2011, which was remounted at the Bush Theatre in London, and published by Oberon Books.

Clare won a Pearson Award for her first full-length play *Crossings* in 2003, which was published and toured the UK in 2005. This led to being Writer in Residence at the West Yorkshire Playhouse in 2004, where she wrote *A Good Man* about a trans man helping his father coming out of prison.

Sophie Ferguson (Costume Designer)

Sophie graduated from the Edinburgh College of Art in 2016, and previously trained in Stage Management at Queen Margaret College.

She has costume supervised at the Traverse regularly since 2015 working on: *What Girls Are Made Of*, *Ulster American*, *Gut*, *Meet Me at Dawn*, *Girl in the Machine*, *Grain in the Blood* and *Milk*.

Recent/current theatre costume work includes: *Interiors* (Vanishing Point); *Jury Play* (Grid Iron/Traverse Theatre); *Tabula Rasa* (Vanishing Point/Scottish Ensemble); *Three Sisters* (Lung Ha).

Set design and assistance: *Expecting Something* (Starcatchers); *The Birthday of the Infanta* (Solar Bear); *Pine Tree, Poggle and Me* (Barrowland Ballet); *A Midsummer Night's Dream* (Theatre Strahl, Berlin); *Penelope Waiting* (State Theatre, Geissen Germany).

Visual Art exhibitions include: *Lines of Enquiry* (Maclaurin Gallery); *Female Instrumentalists* (Porty Artwalk); *BLINK* (Whitespace).

Stephen Jones (Composer & Sound Designer)

Stephen studied English Literature at Glasgow University, and now works as a composer and music producer/sound designer in a variety of contexts.

He records and tours internationally both with his own ensemble Sound of Yell (Chemikal Underground) and as a member of various other groups including Arab Strap and the Alasdair Roberts Trio.

He has composed and performed music for *Where You're Meant To Be* (Chicago Film Festival Documentary of the year 2017) and *A Blemished Code* (BFI/London Film Festival). As a prolific collaborator, he has worked extensively within the Glasgow contemporary art scene: with sound artist Sue Tompkins, experimental filmmaker Luke Fowler and most recently, with artist Victoria Morton on their Hospitalfield commission *What You Do, I Like*.

His theatre sound design and composition credits include *The Devils Larder* (Grid Iron); *The Hairy Ape* (Corcadorca); *In Time of Strife* (National Theatre of Scotland); *MIANN* (Scottish Dance Theatre); *Richard III* (Perth Theatre).

Gareth Nicholls (Director)

Gareth is Associate Director at the Traverse Theatre. His recent shows include *Ulster American, How to Disappear* and *Letters To Morrissey* (Traverse Theatre); the Scottish premiere of Yasmina Reza's *God of Carnage* (Tron Theatre); and the sell-out production of Irvine Welsh's *Trainspotting* (Citizens Theatre).

Other directing credits include: *Blackbird* by David Harrower, *Into That Darkness* by Gitta Sereny, *Vanya* by Sam Holcroft (Citizens Theatre); *Under Milk Wood* by Dylan Thomas (Tron Theatre);

A Gambler's Guide to Dying by Gary McNair (Show & Tell); *Prom* by Oliver Emanuel (Òran Mór); *Educating Ronnie* by Joe Douglas (Utter); *The Tin Forest South West* (National Theatre of Scotland); *Tis Pity She's a Whore, Coriolanus, The Burial at Thebes* (Royal Conservatoire of Scotland).

Gareth has won four Fringe First Awards and was previously Citizens Theatre's Main Stage Director in Residence (2014–16).

Renny Robertson (Lighting Designer)

Renny is Chief Electrician at the Traverse.

Lighting designs for the Traverse include: *Homers, Chic Nerds, The Trestle at Pope Lick Creek, Lazy Bed, Heritage, Right Now*. He has also designed the lighting for various productions of Lung Ha, Room 2 Manoeuvre and Plan B. He has transferred work for the Traverse internationally including: *Bondagers, Damascus, Outlying Islands, Midsummer, The People Next Door*.

Raymond Short (Fight Director)

Raymond choreographed his first fight for his local karate club at the age of 12. He developed his love of drama through school, then moving on to Scottish Youth Theatre and eventually graduating from the Royal Scottish Academy of Music and Drama (Royal Conservatoire of Scotland) in 1994. Since then he has induced thousands of people to injure, maim and kill each other (safely of course!) on stage and screen. He has created violence all over Scotland, the UK and abroad. Raymond is happy to be back once again with the great team at the Traverse.

TRAVERSE THEATRE

About Traverse Theatre Company

Formed in 1963 by a group of passionate theatre enthusiasts, the Traverse Theatre was originally founded to extend the spirit of the Edinburgh festivals throughout the year. Today, under Artistic Director Orla O'Loughlin, the Traverse is proud to deliver its year-round mission of championing creative talent by placing powerful and contemporary theatre at the heart of cultural life – producing and programming urgent and diverse work spanning theatre, dance, performance, music and spoken word.

Through the work it presents, the Traverse aims to both entertain and stir conversation – reflecting the times and provoking crucial debate amongst audiences, inspiring them to ask questions, seek answers and challenge the status quo.

The Traverse has launched the careers of some of the UK's most celebrated writers – David Greig, David Harrower and Zinnie Harris – and continues to discover and support new voices, including Stef Smith, Morna Pearson, Gary McNair and Rob Drummond.

With two custom-built and versatile theatre spaces, the Traverse's home in Edinburgh's city centre holds an iconic status as the theatrical heart of the Edinburgh Festival Fringe every August.

Outside the theatre walls, the Traverse runs an extensive engagement programme, offering audiences of all ages and backgrounds the opportunity to explore, create and develop. Further afield, the Traverse frequently tours internationally and engages in exchanges and partnerships – most recently in India, New Zealand and Quebec.

'The Traverse remains the best new writing theatre in Britain.'
The Guardian

For more information about the Traverse please visit traverse.co.uk

About the Institute for Advanced Studies in the Humanities, University of Edinburgh

Arctic Oil was written during Clare Duffy's Creative Fellowship at the Institute for Advanced Studies in the Humanities (IASH), University of Edinburgh. IASH provides an international, interdisciplinary and autonomous space for discussion and debate. Since its foundation in 1969, more than 1,200 scholars from 66 countries have held Fellowships.

With thanks

The Traverse Theatre extends grateful thanks to all those who generously support our work, including those who prefer their support to remain anonymous.

Traverse Theatre Supporters

Diamond – Alan & Penny Barr, Katie Bradford
Platinum – Angus McLeod, Iain Millar, David Rodgers
Gold – Carola Bronte-Stewart
Silver – Judy & Steve, Bridget M Stevens, Allan Wilson
Bronze – Barbara Cartwright, Alex Oliver & Duncan Stephen

Trusts, Foundations and Grants

Anderson Anderson & Brown Charitable Initiative
Backstage Trust
Bòrd na Gàidhlig
British Council: UK/India 2017
The Cross Trust
The Dr David Summers Charitable Trust
The Evelyn Drysdale Charitable Trust
Fidelio Charitable Trust
The Foyle Foundation
Gannochy Trust
The JMK Trust
Nimar Charitable Trust
Ponton House Trust
The RKT Harris Charitable Trust
The Robert Haldane Smith Charitable Foundation
The Robertson Trust
The Russell Trust
The Souter Charitable Trust
The Steel Charitable Trust
Teale Charitable Trust
Turtleton Charitable Trust
WCH Trust for Children

Traverse Theatre Production Supporters

Allander Print
Cotterell & Co
Paterson SA Hairdressing
Spotlight

Grant Funders

ALBA | CHRUTHACHAIL

Traverse Theatre (Scotland) is a Limited Company (SC076037) and a Scottish Charity (SC002368) with its Registered Office at 10 Cambridge Street, Edinburgh EH1 2ED.

Traverse Theatre – The Company

Linda Crooks	Executive Producer & Joint Chief Executive
Megan Davies-Varnier	Deputy Box Office Manager
Stephen Dennehy	Ticketing & Customer Service Officer
Isobel Dew	Administrator
Anna Docherty	Press & Media Officer
David Drummond	General Manager
Claire Elliot	Deputy Electrician
Danielle Fentiman	Artistic Administrator
Ellen Gledhill	Development Manager
Tom Grayson Morrison	Box Office Manager
Kath Lowe	Front of House Manager
Kevin McCallum	Head of Production
Ruth McEwan	Producer
Lauren McLay	Marketing & Communications Assistant
Suzanne Murray	Bar Café Manager
Victoria Murray	Head of Communications
Carlos Navarro	Head Chef
Gareth Nicholls	Associate Director
Olivia Nolan	Ticketing & Customer Service Officer
Orla O'Loughlin	Outgoing Artistic Director & Joint Chief Executive
Alice Pelan	Finance & Administration Apprentice
Julie Pigott	Head of Finance & Operations
Pauleen Rafferty	Payroll & HR Manager
Sunniva Ramsay	Creative Producer
Renny Robertson	Chief Electrician
Jonathan Rowett	Bar Café Senior Supervisor
Kei Saito	Associate Producer
Tom Saunders	Lighting & Sound Technician
Gary Staerck	Head of Stage
Kyriakos Vogiatzis	Marketing & Campaigns Officer

Also working for the Traverse

Grazyna Adrian, Eleanor Agnew, Charlotte Anderson, Lindsay Anderson, David Bailey, Shellie-Ann Barrowcliffe, Alannah Beaton, Rona Broadhead, Joshua Calder, Emma Campbell, Fiona Campbell, Louise Chan, Hannah Cornish, Stephen Cox, Lauren Crowe, Nicai Cruz, Rachel Cullen, Koralia Daskalaki, Amy Dawson, Molly Duffield, Rachel Duke, Katie Duncan, Sophie Ferguson, Andrew Findlater, Daniel Findlay Carroll, Callum Finlay, Jamie Fleming, Andrew Gannon, Clair Grant, Laura Hawkins, Ella Hendy, Sunny Howie, Catherine Idle, Ian Jackson, Adam James, Nikki Kalkman, Jonathan Kennedy, Sean Langtree, Laura Laria, Fergus Lockie, Catriona Macdonald, Lynsey MacKenzie, Ewa Malicka, Alan Massie, Kieran McCruden, Alison McFarlane, Calum McGowan, Kirsty McIntyre, Steve McMahon, Robin Meldrum, Dino Melia, Edwin Milne, Will Moore, Jamie Morris, Michael Murray,

Clare Duffy

ARCTIC OIL

OBERON BOOKS
LONDON

WWW.OBERONBOOKS.COM

First published in 2018 by Oberon Books Ltd
521 Caledonian Road, London N7 9RH
Tel: +44 (0) 20 7607 3637 / Fax: +44 (0) 20 7607 3629
e-mail: info@oberonbooks.com
www.oberonbooks.com

PB ISBN: 9781786826800
E ISBN: 9781786826794

Cover design by Mihaela Bodlovic

Printed and bound by 4EDGE Limited, Hockley, Essex, UK.
eBook conversion by Lapiz Digital Services, India.

Visit www.oberonbooks.com to read more about all our books and to buy them. You will also find features, author interviews and news of any author events, and you can sign up for e-newsletters so that you're always first to hear about our new releases.

Printed on FSC® accredited paper

10 9 8 7 6 5 4 3 2 1

*For Mrs Henrietta Duffy great grandmother and inspiration
and Mrs Patricia Duffy great mother and inspiration*

Characters

MOTHER

63. Not brought up on The Island, but visited
her grandmother there throughout her life.

DAUGHTER

35. Brought up from 2 on the island. Left age 17.

Place

"The Island" – Imagine somewhere north of the
Shetlands at about 62 degrees latitude. It is a very small
island in the North Sea at the very edge of UK territory
surrounded by oil rich sea beds. Prior to the discovery
of oil and gas the population was approximately 600.
The current population is 3000, 80% of them working
for "The New North Company" since the early 1980s.

Time

Now-ish

MOTHER and DAUGHTER are each in their own spotlight, darkness all around.

DAUGHTER is wearing converse, jogging bottoms and a light knitted jumper, everything bought from a charity shop. MOTHER is wearing expensive 'casual' clothes: skinny jeans and a T-shirt, three diamond rings, a wedding ring, a necklace, diamond earrings, fluffy slippers.

DAUGHTER has a small, long strapped canvas bag and a large rucksack hanging from a shoulder. She puts the rucksack down and takes out a packet of nappies.

MOTHER: *(Raised eyebrow.)* Disposable?

DAUGHTER smiles.

DAUGHTER: Extra absorbent. *(She points to the plus on the packet.)*

That's what the plus means.

Lights open up to show that they are standing by a solid looking wooden door made in panels. MOTHER opens the door onto a pretty grand bathroom. There is a sink, cupboard, toilet and bath with shower. Late evening light spills in from a closed skylight. It is sunset. It won't get darker than Nautical Twilight at this time of the year here.

DAUGHTER: But why would you ever want 'fairly-absorbent'? I mean, for ages I thought the 'plus' meant for plus-sized bums ...you know. Like a size and a half. But no.

MOTHER: Seems like a lot for just two nights.

(She looks and then puts her hands in the rucksack.) And all this as well! How long are you going for?

DAUGHTER: *(Taking a foam changing mat out of the bag.)* I'll be back Sunday evening. You're picking me up. Remember.

MOTHER goes in. Her back is turned for long enough to hide something somewhere. The audience shouldn't particularly notice her do it.

MOTHER: Where is all this going to go?

DAUGHTER checks the time on her phone. She doesn't want to go in.

DAUGHTER: If I hadn't brought extra you'd have moaned there wasn't enough.

MOTHER: Help me will you?

DAUGHTER: I've really got to go.

MOTHER: Only take a moment.

Come on.

DAUGHTER goes in. She puts the changing mat on top of the cupboard and starts putting the nappies, wipes, nappy bags and creams inside it.

MOTHER: Does it always take that long to get him to sleep?

DAUGHTER: That wasn't long!

MOTHER: You were in there for ages.

DAUGHTER: Half an hour.

That's nothing. That's amazing! He's really turned a corner, with the sleeping and

He's such a good little boy really.

MOTHER: He's got you twisted round his little

DAUGHTER: *(Interrupting.)* Jesus. What does that mean!

MOTHER: *(Finishing deliberately.)* Finger.

DAUGHTER: He's a baby mum! Jesus!

MOTHER: But I suppose he is a cheerful wee soul. Most of the time.

DAUGHTER: There. All done. Now.

Got to go.

MOTHER: That's not very convenient is it. Put them on top, where I can get at them.

DAUGHTER: And if I had put them on top they would have been an eye sore right?

DAUGHTER puts them on top of the cupboard.

MOTHER: Are you alright?

DAUGHTER: Fine.

MOTHER: You were such a happy baby.

DAUGHTER: I'm still happy.

MOTHER: You're all at sixes and sevens. Are you sleeping?

DAUGHTER: Oh. You know what I'm like in the summer.

MOTHER: (Pah!) It's not the sun. It's not the light!

DAUGHTER: It is. It's a scientifically proven

MOTHER: *(Interrupting.)* Not for islanders.

DAUGHTER: But I'm not.

MOTHER: Yes you are.

DAUGHTER: Wasn't born here was I?

MOTHER: Are you sleeping at all?

DAUGHTER: Not really. But I feel good. Actually. Maybe a bit too good. A bit wired. A bit. Laa! *(She sings a high note.)*

But who cares. Good is good right. It's the winter that's really hard.

She gathers herself back in. New face.

Thank you. For doing this. It means a lot.

MOTHER: Not a problem.

DAUGHTER: You're the best.

MOTHER: Ella?

DAUGHTER: Why don't you take him up to the fort tomorrow if the weather's good? We walked up along the coast road from the bus stop. It was so beautiful. After the rain, and the sun so low and so…generous. We looked back towards town and I counted four rainbows. Did you see them? And then the sheep!

MOTHER: Sheep?

DAUGHTER: Up on the cliff, by the fort, with sun behind them. All the sheep's wool was shining gold, like halos on medieval angels.

MOTHER: Yes. I know just what you mean.

DAUGHTER: You should take him up there tomorrow.

MOTHER: If it's clement.

DAUGHTER: Do you remember taking me to the fort, to tell me the Viking stories?

MOTHER: Of course.

DAUGHTER: Here. Mum.

I want to give you something.

DAUGHTER takes the necklace off from around her neck and shows it to MOTHER.

MOTHER: Oh. Thank you.

DAUGHTER: Look. That is why I love the arctic, look at it. This is a Dorset bone carving. Look at that face. Can you believe a face like that was carved 2000 years ago? Don't you feel like you're right next to the person who carved it, when you look at it?

I do.

Look at it.

MOTHER squints at the carving. Gets her glasses out to see properly.

In the Arctic nothing decomposes. Did you know that? Not really. I've slept by fireplaces where you could still smell the seal blubber from a meal 900 years ago. Isn't that amazing?!

MOTHER looks and is shocked at the violent, 'scream' face on the pendant.

MOTHER: Dear god!

DAUGHTER: Oh. I know. It's terrifying really isn't it. Sometimes if I look at it for too long I can really freak myself out. Can almost see it moving! But then it does also make me feel better. I suppose because I can see, those people, those ancient people, they obviously had the same feelings as us, living in the dark for months on end and then in the endless days, they were just like us really, and for some reason I do find that comforting.

I want you to have it.

MOTHER: Where is this party?

DAUGHTER: It's a wedding. Mum.

MOTHER: Where is it?

DAUGHTER: Peckham.

MOTHER: London?

DAUGHTER: Yes.

MOTHER: And who are you staying with?

DAUGHTER: Mum we've been through all of this. Don't spoil it.

Take it. Will you? Jesus. I try. I try so hard and you always

MOTHER takes the necklace.

MOTHER: Alright. Alright then.

DAUGHTER: I'm sorry. Mum. I wish. God I wish.

When I was up at the fort I thought. I had this inspiration.
I thought I'll give you the necklace and I'll tell you how
much I love you. Because we never really ever say it, do
we? But I just fuck it up every time.

MOTHER: I don't think you should go.

DAUGHTER: Of course I'm going. I've been planning this for
months. I haven't been off the island in two years. I really
need to get away, just for a few days.

MOTHER: And get some sleep?

DAUGHTER: Yes. I suppose. It will be easier in London. Yes.
Of course. I hadn't thought of that. Added bonus. But
really I just want some fun.

Checks phone. She is ready to go.

MOTHER: What time is the flight?

DAUGHTER: Not *flying*.

MOTHER: How are you going to get to the ferry then?

DAUGHTER: Cab.

MOTHER: And they'll be here…when?

DAUGHTER: Any minute now.

MOTHER: Will they ring the door?

DAUGHTER: I said I'd be at the end of the lane. Now.

MOTHER: Please don't go.

DAUGHTER: What?

MOTHER: Just don't go. You're not ready.

DAUGHTER: Mum. If I don't go. I don't know what I'm going to do!

MOTHER: You're not well.

DAUGHTER: I'm not ill. I'm exhausted and I need a break, a break from, don't make me cry mum. Just help me please for once

MOTHER: You're shaking.

DAUGHTER: No I'm not. Jesus. Mum. Please.

MOTHER puts herself between DAUGHTER and the doorway.

DAUGHTER: You've got my number. Chloe's number. Chloe's mum's number.

MOTHER: It's not really a party you're going to is it?

DAUGHTER: Yes. It's Chloe's wedding.

MOTHER: I know Ella.

DAUGHTER: What? What do you know?

MOTHER: What if you don't come back?

DAUGHTER: Of course I'm going to come back. I'm not going to leave my baby!

MOTHER: What if you die? Do you expect me to bring Sammy up?

DAUGHTER: I'm not going to die! What are you talking about?

MOTHER: I've never interfered before.

DAUGHTER: Ha!

MOTHER: I never said anything when you went on your adventures, even when you were pregnant.

DAUGHTER: What the

MOTHER: I know you were on a boat when you were pregnant.

You can't just behave like before... like a bug in the breeze.

DAUGHTER gives a cry of frustration.

DAUGHTER: Jesus. Get out of my way please.

MOTHER: No.

DAUGHTER: I have to be me again, even if it's just for a few days.

MOTHER: That's the most ridiculous... Who are you? You are a mother. When that little boy cries who are you? You are a mother. But you you know yourself, you're not well.

It's really very common you know. For new mothers. Any new mother, but someone like you,

DAUGHTER: Someone 'like me' what do you mean exactly?!

MOTHER: You know what I mean.

DAUGHTER: I'm not ill, I'm not depressed. I'm bored. I'm tired. I'm desperate for a conversation and a drink and a fucking good time. That's all. Don't fucking gaslight me.

MOTHER: What does that mean?

DAUGHTER: You just can't be bothered to look after Sam. That's what this is.

MOTHER: No. Not at all.

DAUGHTER: What? Does Florence want to play golf tomorrow and you can't because you've got to look after Sam? What a dreadful bore!

MOTHER: You've got a history of

DAUGHTER: I was ill once. You're allowed to go off the rails once. When you're dad dies, when you're a teenager.

MOTHER: You've been off those rails ever since.

DAUGHTER: I'm a healthy, grown woman, I'm a responsible mother.

I'll take him with me. That's all. I'll just have to take him with me.

MOTHER: *(Horrified.)* You can't.

DAUGHTER: I can do what I like with my own son.

MOTHER: I know what you are going to do.

You're not exactly security conscious for a terrorist.

DAUGHTER: Terrorist?!

Mum.

You just don't understand anything do you!

MOTHER: I do. I know you better than you know yourself.

DAUGHTER: Think. Think.

MOTHER: And I'm very sorry, but I can't let you go.

DAUGHTER: Arrogant. Fuck

MOTHER shuts the bathroom door.

MOTHER: I'm really very sorry.

She locks the door.

But I can't let you go and risk your life, when that little boy in there needs his mum.

DAUGHTER: No. Mum!

MOTHER: I'm locking us in until you come to your senses.

DAUGHTER: I've got to go. Mum. The ferry is going to leave in *(Checks phone.)* in an hour. I've got to go. They need me. Chloe needs me. I'm her best friend. I haven't seen her for nearly two years. I'm going to be her maid of honour for fuck's sake. I'm going to wear a dress! A nice dress.

MOTHER: Where is it then?

DAUGHTER: What?

MOTHER: Your fancy dress. You got some heels in that back pack too?

Mother doesn't bother opening the bag to show daughter that there isn't a dress there.

I don't think so.

DAUGHTER: Chloe's buying them for me. They are waiting for me next to a bottle of gin that we're going to drink together and laugh…you know…laugh at shit.

MOTHER: You've got a *boat* that's leaving in an hour. I know! It's in New North harbour now. Right now. Pam's been doing terrorist watch on Instagram all afternoon. Everyone knows.

Not "ferry" my girl. Boat.

DAUGHTER: I'm going to London to see my best friend.

MOTHER: When that boat leaves you'll be safe. You can do what you want then. You can actually go to London. If you really want to.

DAUGHTER: Give me the key.

MOTHER: No.

DAUGHTER: This is ridiculous. Give it to me.

MOTHER: No.

DAUGHTER: I'll break the door down.

MOTHER: And wake up Sammy?

DAUGHTER: Give me the

They struggle.

MOTHER: No.

Her mother slaps her cheek.

DAUGHTER: You. You're the one who's lost their mind.

You can't just lock me up. You can't just make me do what you want.

MOTHER: I can if I'm saving your life.

DAUGHTER: Saving my life?!

But. I'm not going to be in any danger.

MOTHER: You broke your leg once.

DAUGHTER: That was… Jesus –

MOTHER: You're in no state

DAUGHTER: Fuck!

MOTHER: What if you don't come back?

DAUGHTER: I will.

MOTHER: But if you don't come back.

DAUGHTER: I'm coming back.

MOTHER: How will he cope without his mum?

DAUGHTER: Nothing is going to happen.

You can't just lock the door.

MOTHER: I can.

MOTHER eats the key. DAUGHTER stares for a moment in disbelief.

DAUGHTER: Shit.

You have lost it. You have totally lost the plot. I wouldn't leave Sam with you now if you paid me.

MOTHER shows her empty mouth.

Fuck you!

DAUGHTER starts seriously trying to bash the door open with her shoulder.

MOTHER watches her.

MOTHER: You can't get out like that.

DAUGHTER runs at the door and tries to smash it open.

MOTHER: That's oak that door.

Cost my Nanna a great deal that wood.

DAUGHTER steps back to take another run at it.

MOTHER: Dragged it up from the beach herself she did.

DAUGHTER runs at the door and bashes it.

DAUGHTER: Aaaaaaaaaagh!

MOTHER: In the middle of the night.

DAUGHTER steps back again and runs at it again.

DAUGHTER: Grrrrrrrrgh!

DAUGHTER stops. Breathing heavily now. Doubled over.

MOTHER: They saved the wood while the storms were still raging.

DAUGHTER: *(Out of breath.)* Yes. When people were drowning. When they could have been saving drowning people.

DAUGHTER remembers she has a penknife in her bag and starts to look for it in her bag.

MOTHER: Rubbish. As if. As if you could save…

You should know better. Listening to local gossip.

DAUGHTER can't find her penknife.

DAUGHTER: What the fuck?

MOTHER: You've always reminded me of her… stubborn as a Shetland pony.

DAUGHTER: You've taken my penknife!

MOTHER: No.

DAUGHTER: You must have taken it.

DAUGHTER rampages through the bathroom looking for the knife.

The doorbell rings.

DAUGHTER: That's them. That's them. Oh no. Oh shit. No.

DAUGHTER looks for her mobile phone. She can't find that either. She looks at her mum. It is in her mum's hands.

DAUGHTER: Mum. Give me my phone back. Please. I won't go. You win. Please.

MOTHER: I'm not stupid.

The doorbell starts to ring insistently.

DAUGHTER: *(Trying to pacify her.)* No. No. You're not. You're not stupid. You just don't understand.

MOTHER: I understand well enough.

DAUGHTER: Give me the phone mum.

MOTHER: Sammy needs you.

DAUGHTER: This *is* for him. *Please!*

MOTHER drops the phone into the toilet and flushes.

DAUGHTER: No. No. No.

She rushes to the toilet and struggles to find and then take out the wet and for now useless mobile phone trying to dry it on the towels.

MOTHER: If you put it in dry rice it will be fine in a day or two. Flo says.

The doorbell stops ringing. DAUGHTER still drying the phone in a towel looks around the room to see what other routes of escape there might be. She considers the skylight. It's a possibility. She pulls the cord to open it and jumps up to shout outside.

She catches a hand on the ledge and tries to pull herself up. She can't quite make it.

DAUGHTER: Wait. Please. Please wait. Just. Wait.

Silence.

Seabirds. Waves.

DAUGHTER turns to look at her mother.

DAUGHTER: I hate you.

MOTHER: Don't be silly.

DAUGHTER: *(Listens.)* I can hear Sammy.

MOTHER: No.

DAUGHTER: What do you mean "no"? I can hear my son crying.

MOTHER takes out a baby monitor hidden in a cupboard or draw. She turns it on. The sound of a baby's snoring can be heard now through the monitor.

MOTHER: He's fine. Listen.

And you said yourself. He sleeps through now. He'll be asleep for eight hours still.

He's fine.

BABY does a short cry.

DAUGHTER: See.

DAUGHTER bangs again on the door trying to wake Sammy up.

DAUGHTER: Sammy!

There's then a big sigh and the baby clearly settles again to easy light snoring.

DAUGHTER: Fuck it.

MOTHER: You would use your own child just to get what you want.

DAUGHTER: Shut up!

MOTHER: I can't believe that you would seriously think of taking a baby on a terrorist boat.

DAUGHTER: Shut up!

MOTHER: Or were you always going to abandon him, were you even planning to come back?!

DAUGHTER kicks the wall and hurts her foot.

DAUGHTER: Ow.

MOTHER: And you say you're not depressed.

DAUGHTER: No need to look so fucking smug. This isn't a joke you know.

MOTHER: I know.

MOTHER takes out a thermos of tea and a packet of biscuits.

MOTHER: Don't use that language Ella. It puts my nerves on edge.

DAUGHTER: Fuck. Fuck. Fuck.

MOTHER: Calm down. Stop acting like such a ... fucking child.

The look at each other for a moment.

DAUGHTER: I know you don't understand. I know you don't believe. I understand why you use words like terrorism. Really. I do. But. But.

Mum. Can you try to imagine what you are doing, what the consequences are going to be. I have a job. I've got a role… we are a team. They need me. You are putting lives at risk by stopping me being there to help them.

MOTHER: So it is dangerous.

DAUGHTER: Now. Now that I'm not there. Now that they are missing someone.

MOTHER: Don't you think Sammy is going to miss you. Isn't he your first responsibility?

DAUGHTER: This is for Sam. For him. His children. Your great grandchildren. What use will oil be, when the Earth is dead?

MOTHER: Bullshit. When I was young it was the atom bomb. Then it was the millennium bug and now its global warming. Some people. Certain people, of a particular disposition, will see apocalypse on every horizon.

Beat.

DAUGHTER: Okay. You've made your point. I won't go. Fine. They've gone. I've missed the boat. You win.

Will you let me out now so I can check on him? I just want to check on him. Please.

MOTHER: You just saw me swallow the key didn't you?

DAUGHTER: But that was a fake one wasn't it? A dummy key. A double? Or you put it into your other hand. You haven't actually swallowed the only key that will let us out when there's a baby on his own in another room. You wouldn't be that crazy would you?

MOTHER: He'll be fine.

DAUGHTER: How do you know?

MOTHER: He's asleep.

DAUGHTER: He could have a fever.

MOTHER: He's fine.

DAUGHTER: But he could have a fever.

MOTHER: He's fine.

DAUGHTER: But he's teething and he could have a fever and it can be really dangerous if they get very hot very quickly and you don't get the temperature down.

MOTHER: I know and he's fine.

She holds up a cup.

Do you want one?

DAUGHTER: You think this is a joke? That my life is a joke?

MOTHER: The exact opposite.

I can't any risks.

…

Besides. I'm very regular. We should get the key back at around seven, I should think.

And just in case I've asked Flo to come and stay the night. She'll let herself in.

DAUGHTER: Flo. Fucking Flo.

MOTHER: You love Flo.

DAUGHTER: Not right now I don't.

MOTHER: Why do you want to put yourself at risk? That's what I don't understand.

DAUGHTER: It's what I'm good at. It is what I do.

MOTHER: But why does it have to be so dangerous?

DAUGHTER: The way we live every day is dangerous. We're taking such an epic risk with the earth we can't even see it.

MOTHER: Maybe we can't see it because it isn't there.

DAUGHTER: Is it your total ignorance that allows you to be so fucking arrogant?

MOTHER: I read. I am informed. You're pretty arrogant assuming you know what I know.

DAUGHTER: I know the Arctic is beautiful. I've been there. If it wasn't for me you'd never leave the peninsula.

MOTHER: Ha! Really beautiful! … Nothing but snow and ice. Oh look over there it's soooo white and over there look ooooh it's completely white too and there and there and look here… it's nothing by whiteness with plenty of cold thrown in for good measure! *(Laughs.)*

DAUGHTER: You've no idea. It's magical. In the summer there's so much life, migrating caribou, and geese, and fields of tiny bright moss flowers and in winter of course it's tough, but there's such warmth, a way of thinking, of being together you never get with folk here.

MOTHER: Well. I never imagined. Garden of Eden and communist utopia all rolled into one is it!

DAUGHTER: I don't even know what you think that means.

MOTHER: You sound like a tourist Ella. It's good to have freedom. It's good to not have to do what everyone else does. You would be the first person to get out, and not look back, if it was your actual home. Where you actually came from.

DAUGHTER: When the Arctic ice melts half this island will be under the sea.

MOTHER: Rubbish.

DAUGHTER: How ironic that the oil that built all the roads and the sports centers thirty years ago is going to wash them all away by the time Sammy is eighty. If we don't

MOTHER: Total and utter rubbish.

DAUGHTER: You're so used to seeing the rigs here, you can't see how monstrous, how abhorrent they truly are.

MOTHER: Abhorrent!

DAUGHTER: But at least this isn't the Arctic.

MOTHER: What's so special about the sea a few hundred miles north of here? It's just the same. It's just water.

DAUGHTER: There has to be somewhere that's perfect, that's clean.

MOTHER: Why? Nowhere is perfect or clean. We're dirty. We're messy. We die. That's life. But what we do have, what we do have is our family. They come first. Have to.

DAUGHTER: Some things are bigger than family. We're part of a bigger family than

MOTHER: So you *would* leave him behind. Be honest. All this 'saving the world' it's not the real story is it. I know you. Tell the truth.

Beat.

DAUGHTER: Okay. Yes. I'm bored. I'm so bored here. I'm bored of being a boring mum. Yes.

MOTHER: Ha!

DAUGHTER: Yes. You are right. Since they asked me I've been dreaming day and night of being on the boat again. Being the first one to spot the flare. Hoping to be the first one on the boat to say, "There she blows!" That red flare in the white sky, it's almost like a whale plume. But not thoughtful like a whale breathing in and out...it just breathes fire out-out-out.

Being the first to see that new rig on the horizon, already bits falling off it.

Of course I want to tear it down. I want to destroy it and all the others. I want to throw my body into the world and make something change... or die trying.

MOTHER: Oh Ella.

DAUGHTER: I thought this was what you wanted to hear?

MOTHER: No.

DAUGHTER: Mum. Two years I've been here, no sex, no drugs and no fucking fun. And watching the insanity, the chaos getting worse and worse! They are deleting scientific data mum. Deleting it. How are we supposed to research, how are we supposed to know anything if basic factual records are destroyed?

MOTHER: I don't think that's

DAUGHTER: *(Interrupting.)* And yes. I want to be part of the battle. I imagine it as I'm holding him in my arms every night. I imagine seeing that great island fortress getting quickly clearer and as we approach the smell of her getting stronger and stronger. And it makes my heart pound.

MOTHER: Listen. Dear. Just try to...try to breathe.

DAUGHTER: You don't expect to notice the smell of things so much at sea.

The air at sea especially in the Arctic is quite different to on land. As you get closer to land you smell the world, your old home, the fat of the land. I didn't understand that expression before. But you can smell all the fat of all the people cooking and eating and sweating and breathing. If you've been far enough away from land for long enough you notice it. In the Arctic the air is so sweet. It seems impossible at first, that sweetness, and then you become used to it and you don't smell it anymore.

The Arctic air is so sweet and then when you smell the rig, it's like you can smell a dog fight, a bear fight. You can smell the emptied bowls of terrified animals.

You can smell the iron, the rust, the men and women, their food and their sweat. You can smell the helicopters and the oil.

Those workers are doing twelve hour shifts through months and months of night. Man-made disasters always happen in the middle of night. Because we are animals who have evolved on a planet that orbits the fucking sun and it's in every atom of our being to turn to the sun, to be ruled by the sun. We can't trust ourselves to operate oil rigs in these environments. It's so inevitable that terrible mistakes will be made in the short run and in the long run...well..they just shouldn't be there. It's so wrong.

And yes sometimes I do wonder. What can I hope to achieve? Hasn't it all gone already. Hasn't the film already finished and we're just watching the credits? Why don't I just

give up hope.

MOTHER touches DAUGHTER's arm gently.

MOTHER: Ella.

DAUGHTER: But then I think fuck that!

DAUGHTER snatches her MOTHER's mobile phone from her hand.

DAUGHTER: I can still make the boat.

She starts to tap in a number.

I told you you should put a code on your phone.

MOTHER: Who are you calling?

DAUGHTER: The police.

MOTHER: No you're not.

DAUGHTER: You've imprisoned me against my will and I'm calling the police, because that's what they are there for.

MOTHER: Don't try to bother the Police with this. They've got real things to deal with.

DAUGHTER: This is real.

MOTHER: You're not in any danger. And anyway, you think Mike is going to believe you over me? I've known Mike all his life.

DAUGHTER: *(On the phone in response to "Which service do you need?".)* Police.

I'm being held against my will.

My mother.

I'm.

MOTHER: And there's no phone signal on this side of the house. It's just wifi. You could Facetime with Mike, I suppose. His mobile number is in there under Mike Policeman.

It'll only take him what, an hour and a half to get here. If he leaves straight away.

DAUGHTER: *(Looks at MOTHER for a moment.)*

Fuck.

…

I could message my friends.

MOTHER: What friends?!

DAUGHTER: /I have friends.

MOTHER: You have friends all over the world. But you know no one here.

DAUGHTER: God. I know *everyone* here.

MOTHER: You're no better than anybody else, you know.

DAUGHTER still has her MOTHER's phone. She puts it inside her bra and starts to search again for the penknife.

DAUGHTER: So you've been going through my things. For how long? What? You've been reading my emails? My diary?

I wanted to trust you.

But you always do this to me.

Eventually you always cut me down at the fucking knees.

DAUGHTER looks at the big tubs of cream and bubble bath on the side of the bath and then at her mum.

MOTHER: I was worried about you.

DAUGHTER: Really!

She opens the tubs and uses a pen maybe to feel around inside.

MOTHER: You won't find anything in there.

DAUGHTER: You've put it *somewhere.*

MOTHER: I first noticed you weren't right a few weeks ago.

DAUGHTER: Why? What did I do oh sweet queen of insight and perception?

MOTHER: You stopped singing, at the bookbug.

DAUGHTER: I did not.

MOTHER: You always used to sing all the songs. But then you stopped singing, "A Big Red Bus".

She has found the penknife in a big tub of face cream.

DAUGHTER: Oh my god.

Look! Look at what you did.

How long have you been planning this?

She waves the cream covered knife in her mum's face then flicks and wipes the cream on the floor of the bath.

MOTHER: It was the Big Red Bus song. You know.

She does the actions.

"A big red bus, a big red bus,

Mini mini mini and a big red bus.

Ferrari. Ferrari."

DAUGHTER finishes wiping the knife clean and pulls out the screwdriver attachment on the penknife. She starts unscrewing the hinges on the door. They are very old and stiff.

DAUGHTER: Yes. I am aware of the propaganda to which you refer.

MOTHER: It's just a children's song.

DAUGHTER: *(Deliberately winding her mum up.)* It's the normalization of capitalist earth rape.

MOTHER laughs and stops quickly.

MOTHER: You're joking.

DAUGHTER: No!

MOTHER: Well I didn't raise you to spout ideology parrot fashion. I raised you to have your own mind. Your own brain and that…that… just fell out of your silly mouth…

DAUGHTER: Stop.

MOTHER: Rape?!

DAUGHTER: Not singing at Bookbug?!

MOTHER: It's just an example, one small example of your increasingly extreme and unpredictable behaviour.

DAUGHTER: I didn't put a banner over the library door did I? I didn't occupy Bookbug. I just didn't sing one song. And really, given what's fucking going on, right now, I think it's a remarkable act of self-restraint to not shout and scream

She can't stop herself actually screaming

"What do you think you're all doing?!!!"

DAUGHTER's hand slips and she hurts her hand with the screwdriver.

Ow!

DAUGHTER bends over with her hand between her legs.

Fuck.

MOTHER looks around and improvising, gives a nappy to DAUGHTER.

MOTHER: I'm your mother. I know you better than you know yourself.

DAUGHTER takes it and holds it to her hand to soak up the blood.

MOTHER finds a plaster and hands it over. DAUGHTER takes it and puts it on.

So. Yes. That was what made me suspect something wasn't quite right.

Then I heard that you're not sleeping.

DAUGHTER: You heard?

MOTHER: Yes.

DAUGHTER: Jesus. What does that mean?

I mean. Who told you that? As you've already pointed out. I don't have any friends.

MOTHER: We still care you know. Even if you don't talk to us.

DAUGHTER: You mean you got my neighbours to spy on me?

MOTHER: It's not spying.

DAUGHTER: I think it is. Who was it?

MOTHER: I go into town and people cross the street to tell me they can see your lights on, can hear your music.

DAUGHTER: People? Jemma? Auntie Carol? Ted. Arthur? They're not 'people' are they? They are them. New North Oil Company arse kissers everyone.

MOTHER: They love you. We all do.

DAUGHTER: There ought to be a law against it.

MOTHER: You don't want to end up in the hospital do you. When you had your little turn before people crossed in the other direction to avoid talking to me.

DAUGHTER: I don't even know why I'm talking to you. Because every time I engage with you on some level I'm also confirming your position.

DAUGHTER starts again trying to unscrew the door.

DAUGHTER: And stop trying to make out like I'm the one with a mental condition. You've just eaten a key!

DAUGHTER stops working on the door and looks at MOTHER.

This isn't a joke. You're not playing a game.

MOTHER: No. You're here and you're safe. That's all that matters. Isn't it?

DAUGHTER: It's not safe here!

DAUGHTER starts again trying to unscrew the door.

MOTHER: Of course it is.

And I'm sorry Ella, but it's the only room in the house with a lock and I had to do something.

DAUGHTER: I thought you were going to take it off.

MOTHER: I just never seem to get around to it.

DAUGHTER: What if *you* had a heart attack and the door was locked?

MOTHER: You'd call 999 wouldn't you?

If you were here of course.

…

Someone would.

DAUGHTER stops again and looks at her MOTHER with a sudden insight.

DAUGHTER: Is this really about me?

MOTHER: Yes dear.

DAUGHTER: Nothing's bothering *you*?

MOTHER: You!

DAUGHTER: Apart from me.

MOTHER: No. I'm fine.

DAUGHTER: Really? Because you've been a bit quiet at bookbug yourself recently. You know. I thought I spotted a tear in your eye singing Three Little Ducks.

MOTHER: No. Well. That's just normal.

A beat.

DAUGHTER: I hate it in here. I don't know how you can stand it. Why didn't you turn it in to a study or a bedroom or something? Change the fucking shower curtain at least.

MOTHER: That's not the same one.

DAUGHTER: Really. Looks exactly the same.

MOTHER: Your father is everywhere in this house, for me. It's not just in here. I know it's different for you. I'm sorry about that. I really am. I did think. But I had no choice.

DAUGHTER looks at MOTHER.

DAUGHTER: You have a folder somewhere with it all planned out don't you? Some kind of schedule…list?

MOTHER: Yes.

DAUGHTER: And you didn't consider talking to me, all those weeks ago when you first noticed the great, 'Big Red Bus boycott'?

MOTHER: No. Well. Yes. But I just didn't know how to.

The mobile phone alarms. DAUGHTER looks at her MUM's phone. She is full of cold fear.

DAUGHTER: No.

MOTHER: What?

DAUGHTER: You follow us?

MOTHER: What's happening?

DAUGHTER: Oh god. Oh god. No.

She is shaking. Scared to look. Finding it hard to breath.

MOTHER: What?

DAUGHTER plays an audio clip. We hear the sound of a confusion of French, Canadian French, US, Russian and English voices shouting. "Let go" and "I can't let go." "Let me go." Waves and wind. Then several gun shots. MOTHER watches over DAUGHTER's shoulder.

MOTHER: You're being shot at.

DAUGHTER: Yes.

MOTHER: At the new rig.

DAUGHTER: Yes.

MOTHER: But. I thought. You couldn't have got there by now.

DAUGHTER: I was supposed to be on the supply ship. They left a week ago.

MOTHER: Oh.

Is it the Russians? You do know where you stand with the Russians. They don't muck about that lot.

DAUGHTER: I have to get out.

DAUGHTER manages to unscrew one screw of two door hinges. She throws it into the bath.

There is the sound of a key turning in a lock downstairs. Mother and daughter hear it and freeze. They listen to a door opening and closing downstairs. A kettle is switched on. Someone is making a cup of tea.

DAUGHTER: Who's that?

MOTHER: I told you. I asked Flo to stay the night. Just in case.

DAUGHTER: *(Starts banging on the door and shouting.)* "Florence. Florence up here. Quick. Please. Something's happened. I need your help. Please Flo. Quick.

DAUGHTER beats on the door. She screams

DAUGHTER: Flo. I have to get out Flo.

Please. Turn on the telly. Something terrible is happening.

MOTHER: Don't do anything Flo. We're all right in here.

DAUGHTER: No. We're not at "all right" in here.

Florence. Remember. This is me. This is Ella. I am your god daughter. I'm being kept in here against my will.

MOTHER: For your own good.

DAUGHTER: But you can do the right thing Florence. You can be a hero Flo.

MOTHER: Don't listen to her Flo.

DAUGHTER: Florence. There's a key. Downstairs in the kitchen, in the cupboard, where she keeps the nice plates, there is a biscuit tin, a Christmas biscuit tin… and in there you will find a key, on a ring with a wooden star.

MOTHER: Walk away Flo.

DAUGHTER: Flo. Listen to me. This isn't a joke. This is really serious. Sam's father, his dad, is being shot at right now.

MOTHER looks at DAUGHTER. She doesn't know if this is true or not.

DAUGHTER: I have to get out. I have to find out what is going on. This changes everything.

MOTHER: Flo. It's even more important that we keep her out of harm's way now. If this is true.

Sam's dad?

DAUGHTER: Yes.

MOTHER: Florence. Do not open that door. We are alright in here. If you let her out now she'll do something desperate and I'll never have this chance again, will I? Listen to me. Do not be tempted to open that door.

DAUGHTER: This is the life of the father of my child. I have to find out what is happening. I should be on my way there right now and instead I'm stuck in this fucking bathroom.

Please Flo. If I promise not to go anywhere. I just want to see my baby. Flo. I need to. He is my baby.

And his Father is…

I don't even know. We don't know anything.

He could be hurt. Dead.

(To MOTHER.) How long are you going to keep me in here?

Flo. If he wakes up, he will be scared and you won't be able to comfort him. Only me or my mum can do that. And

Also.

You couldn't know this Flo. Because I hadn't told mum. But he needs some medicine if he wakes up in the night. He has asthma attacks sometimes if he gets scared in the night.

MOTHER: She's definitely lying about that Florence.

DAUGHTER: It's true Flo. Are you really willing to take that chance? With a baby's life?

It's too late to reason with mum. But you, you are still rational. Aren't you? You can still do the right thing. You can open this door. You can let me out. Let me out.

MOTHER: Don't do it Flo.

DAUGHTER: Let me out!

She bangs on the door again.

MOTHER: There's nothing wrong with Sammy. Go and check him. Check to see if he has a temperature. *(MOTHER looks at the monitor to see the temperature.)* It's only 20 degrees in his room.

DAUGHTER: Out.

MOTHER: He is breathing normally. We can hear that on the monitor in here. Just check his temperature and then if it's ok. You can give the signal.

DAUGHTER: *(Banging on the door.)* Out. Out. Out.

There is a knock on the door from outside. A 'password' knock.

MOTHER: Ok. We'll wait.

MOTHER and DAUGHTER look at each other, waiting to hear back from Florence.

DAUGHTER: I don't know why I even considered, why I have ever, at any stage entertained the idea that your feelings were in anyway significant in the decisions I make about my life.

MOTHER: What?

DAUGHTER: I'm going to leave the island. For good.

MOTHER: *(Holds her breasts briefly.)* Really?

DAUGHTER: Yes.

MOTHER: How will you afford

DAUGHTER: *(Interrupting.)* I've been offered a job. A really good job that I really want to do. It will pay for a nursery and a place to live and

MOTHER: Well. That's great news darling. Where is this job?

DAUGHTER: Down south.

MOTHER: *(Makes a joke of it..)* Not Shetland?!

DAUGHTER: Birmingham.

You didn't find that out in all your snooping, with all of your spies on every corner?

MOTHER: It's just an offer at the moment. You haven't decided.

DAUGHTER: I *just* decided to say "yes".

MOTHER: No. But. When will I see you?

DAUGHTER: When you come and visit. You can call me and make arrangements on the telephone.

There is a coded knock again on the door.

MOTHER: Thank you Flo.

A last series of knocks.

MOTHER: See. It's all fine.

He's asleep. He's fine. We're all going to be fine.

…

Help yourself to a drink Flo.

DAUGHTER: No. Flo. Don't have 'a drink'. I don't want the only person able to look after Sam smashed on Mum's Ardbeg!

She's scrolling through the twitter feed anxiously.

MOTHER: I think you should still consider staying here. At least until Sammy is school age. This is such a good environment for a child to grow up in. I can help you, financially. You don't need to work. Not like me. Enjoy these years. They go so quickly. And

DAUGHTER takes a rope out of her bag and ties it to the straps.

MOTHER: What are you doing?

DAUGHTER: I'm going to get my son and get out of here.

DAUGHTER stands on the edge of the bath and throws the rope up to the skylight aiming to use the bag as an anchor against the window. It lands outside the skylight.

MOTHER: I wish your father was here, just now. He was so much better at reasoning with you. Why did you always listen to him so much more than me?

Why do I have to do everything on my own?

DAUGHTER pulls on the rope and it falls back down into the bathroom. She gets down and starts trying to land the rope again.

DAUGHTER: Dad was a depressed alcoholic who basically killed himself by proxy.

MOTHER: Your father wasn't depressed.

DAUGHTER: But he was an alcoholic?!

MOTHER: Well of course he drank too much. But everyone does. It doesn't mean.

DAUGHTER: He hated living here. He hated the extreme light. He hated New North Oil.

You're the one who insisted we stay in this ridiculous house.

She tries her weight on the rope again.

MOTHER: Is that really what you think?

DAUGHTER: Yes.

The rope falls back in.

DAUGHTER: Fuck.

MOTHER: Well. You don't know everything. You were only 16. You didn't know everything that was going on. Despite what you think, I do actually protect you. He had a heart attack the year before. We didn't tell you because we didn't want to worry you. But he had stopped drinking and he was much much better. Hopeful. Fun to be with.

DAUGHTER: Oh my god. He died in my arms. I could smell the whisky on his breath.

MOTHER: You would just say anything to hurt me. I know. But there's no need to make up such wicked lies.

Why are you lying to me like this Ella? You never used to be such a liar.

DAUGHTER: I'm not lying. That's what I remember. It's what I know.

He took the company's money and shut up about health and safety and he never ever forgave himself. You know that. I know that. The whole fucking island knows that. In its silence. In its fear. Because what would happen if everyone started telling the truth?

MOTHER: Truth. You wouldn't know the truth if it farted in your face.

DAUGHTER: Maybe there would be less drinking, less suicide and less fucking fatal "accidents".

MOTHER: So this is revenge? You blame me, us and you're trying to terrorize us.

DAUGHTER: No. Mum. I'm trying to save us. I'm here. I'm one of 'us'. Aren't I?! I am terrified. All the time. I'm trying to

She throws the rope again. It falls back down for a third time.

DAUGHTER: Fuck it.

Okay. What about your real deep down reasons then.
Why are you like this? Is it because you are ashamed?

MOTHER: Ashamed?!

DAUGHTER: You all of you…you've spent all the money,
taken all the stuff and now there's nothing left for us
except the mess. If that was my legacy I wouldn't want to
believe it either.

MOTHER: /My God you are so spoilt.

DAUGHTER: And you can't deal with how much you've
fucked up, so you

MOTHER: You've been so spoilt.

DAUGHTER: You just deny/the facts.

MOTHER: /What a luxury to be wasting all your talents on pet
projects. What a luxury to have the state pay for your food
and heat and home.

DAUGHTER: Your willful dumb self-serving ignorance makes
me so angry.

MOTHER: Do you have hot running water? Does Sammy not
have a bath every single night?

DAUGHTER: That's not the

MOTHER: My mum did piece work to feed us. I didn't do A
levels because I had to get a job.

DAUGHTER: You

MOTHER: Me and my sisters had a tin bath in front of the fire
every Saturday night, /whether we needed it or not.

DAUGHTER: / *(Mimicking the well-worn phrase.)* "Whether you needed it or not".

MOTHER: You have no idea.

And I had to go, go to evening class to study to be able to get the promotion that paid for you to get all these big ideas, flouncing around in your rarified poverty, holes in your clothes and rats in your hair and no bloody clue. I was the one who paid for your privilege.

I object to being told what to think and what to do by my own daughter. This is a democracy.

DAUGHTER: Ha!

MOTHER: I shouldn't have to worry about what I say. I shouldn't have to worry about a knock on the door in the middle of night because of something I said, or thought even. It's a free country.

DAUGHTER: You don't object. You shut your eyes and put your fingers in your ears.

It's here. Hundreds of thousands of people are already dying

MOTHER: Where?

DAUGHTER: Bangladesh. China. India....

MOTHER: There will always be poor people.

DAUGHTER: *(Outraged.)* What?

MOTHER: You and Sammy will be okay. Thanks to me.

DAUGHTER: Get out of my way. You are a selfish, heartless, blind old woman. *You* should be shot at, for saying that. You should be shot.

The sound of the twitter feed.

DAUGHTER looks at the phone.

DAUGHTER: Oh. No. No. No.

MOTHER: Ella.

DAUGHTER: Get out of my way!

DAUGHTER pushes MOTHER to the side roughly, so that she can try again to get out of the skylight. Her MOTHER falls and hurts herself. DAUGHTER looks at her. She gets up onto the side of the bath and starts to throw the rope again. She hooks the bag against the open skylight and tests the weight. It holds.

Her MOTHER gets to her feet shakily.

MOTHER: Don't go. Please. I've got to stop you. I've got to tell you.

DAUGHTER: Let me go.

MOTHER grabs her DAUGHTER around the legs. DAUGHTER kicks one foot loose, holding her balance with the rope, kicks at her MOTHER to ward her off, then misses her footing on the edge of the bath, steps back and slips on the cream and screws inside the bath.

The lights flicker.

DAUGHTER hits her head on the side of the bath then slumps out of view.

MOTHER stares for a moment in shock.

MOTHER: Ella.

Ella. Are you?

Oh Ella.

MOTHER gets into the bath and tries to pick her DAUGHTER up into her arms. DAUGHTER is floppy. There is blood on MOTHER's hands.

MOTHER: No, no, no.

...

No.

I'm not having this. I refuse.

Wake up.

Wake up!

You're not going to get away with this Ella. You just stop it now.

Ella. Ella. Wake up!

MOTHER suddenly believes her DAUGHTER is dead and bursts into tears.

Baby starts crying.

Blackout.

Baby stops crying.

The sound of waves crashing.

Lights up. The light from the skylight has become darker. The door is open.

MOTHER is still in the bath with DAUGHTER in her arms. She is stroking her.

When you were a baby I listened to you breathing at night. I imagined the air passing through your lungs, over your tongue and gums, through your nose. I imagined what I would do if I fell asleep and then went to you in the morning and found you weren't breathing. I imagined what I would do: holding you in my arms, ringing 999, shouting, panicking. I imagined your head flopping in my arms and the unbearable

Unbearable

The cry. The sound of…the unbearable

I imagined you falling from our boat when you were a toddler. Slipping out of the life jacket. I imagined jumping in the water to save you too late. And heaving you back up and not being able to and then just holding you and sinking the two of us into the sea and screaming the water into my own lungs and that being the end. But I knew I wouldn't. I knew I wouldn't. I knew I would get you to land and I would bring you back to life. I would do the impossible. I would give you my life and I would go and that would be a good deal. Wouldn't it.

It would be the only possible. The only bearable deal.

I don't believe in god. Do you?

I will make a god to bring you back.

I will go out on to the sand like they did before and build the god with the rocks and the sand and I will burn myself as an offering to my new god and you will be saved and I will be happy.

The only possible happy.

I imagined when you were away. You know. You know how you were away all those years. I learnt how to live with that. I thought I had. But I hadn't. I just didn't think about you. I hardened my heart. Because I couldn't live with the pain.

You can't comprehend the death of your child. Can you.

Can you?

Answer me.

…

I imagined you coming back in the middle of the night and getting into bed with me just like you did when you were a little girl. I would wake up and imagine I could hear the phone ringing. I would actually hear the phone ring and pick it up and there you were, your voice all easy breazy, like nothing had happened,

Sometimes it was your Dad. Sometimes I would hear your dad's voice on the phone telling me you had been found.

…

…

…

Mum.

I want my mum.

You can't do this. You can't. You have a whole life ahead. You have Sam to bring up. You have a life. If you live. I will go instead. I will die and you will live with Sam.

Let *me* go.

Let *me* go.

DAUGHTER opens her eyes and looks at MOTHER.

MOTHER: There you are. Now. Stay still. The doctor's coming. You had a wee bump on the head. But you're going to be fine. You'll see.

DAUGHTER: *(Not moving.)* What happened? Sam. Where's Sam?

She struggles to sit up.

Looks around.

Remembers.

MOTHER: You're not supposed to move. Not until the ambulance gets here.

You tripped.

DAUGHTER: Oh. Yes. I remember.

…

You pushed me.

MOTHER: Of course I didn't.

DAUGHTER: Yes. You pushed me.

MOTHER: I was trying to stop you falling.

DAUGHTER starts to sit up carefully. Head dizzy.

MOTHER: How do you feel?

DAUGHTER: Dizzy.

MOTHER: How many fingers?

MOTHER holds up two fingers.

DAUGHTER doesn't engage with this.

MOTHER: Florence has gone to get a doctor.

You were

You've been unconscious for a bit.

DAUGHTER: How long?

MOTHER: A while. An hour maybe. Stay still.

DAUGHTER: What's happened? I saw Ben's name. He was
one of the ones who were shot. I have to find out.

Daughter is unsuccessfully trying to get to her feet. She gives
up and rests for a moment.

DAUGHTER: I don't feel well. I feel awful.

MOTHER: I thought.

*DAUGHTER feels for the mobile phone and sees it in her mum's
hands.*

MOTHER: Don't worry about that now.

DAUGHTER: Give me the phone.

*MOTHER hands it to her. DAUGHTER squints at it. Gives the
phone back.*

DAUGHTER: Tell me.

MOTHER: *(Scans/scrolls through the twitter read.)* There is more
news.

Four arrested. They're being treated in prison.

DAUGHTER: Treated?

MOTHER: Two of them were injured. Shot. But not. Not…
dead. They're all alive. That's good news isn't it. Four of
them are being kept in prison, until the trial.

You've got to stay positive.

DAUGHTER: What trial?

MOTHER: The lawyers are saying it will never come to court.

DAUGHTER: What?

MOTHER: They're not dead. That's the main thing. I mean.
They could have been. They could have been shot dead.

DAUGHTER: Who? Who!!!

MOTHER: *(Reads from phone.)* Niles Jackson, Benjamin Obi,
Sonja Rance and Hannah Zinker are being held on a
prison island in the Arctic Ocean.

DAUGHTER: Ben.

MOTHER: That could have been you.

DAUGHTER: I'm not fit enough to climb anymore. Look at
me.

I was going to see Ben.

MOTHER: Thought you said lives depended on you.

DAUGHTER: What happens if you don't eat?

MOTHER: Just taking them a few tins of pinapple were you?

DAUGHTER: Yes.

MOTHER: Not going for any oats of your own then?

DAUGHTER: Mum!

MOTHER: Well. I'd buy that sooner than 'saving the earth'.

DAUGHTER: Just as well I'm not selling you anything then
isn't it.

MOTHER: …

So. This "Ben"

DAUGHTER: You have met. At the hospital. He was there at
the birth.

MOTHER: …

I thought he was just a friend. Why didn't you say anything?

DAUGHTER: You didn't ask.

MOTHER: You told me there wasn't a father.

DAUGHTER: No.

MOTHER: Yes.

DAUGHTER: I didn't say anything and you never asked. You assumed. I assume you assumed.

DAUGHTER struggles to sit up holding her head.

MOTHER: Are you still… Do you love him?

DAUGHTER: I don't know. Maybe. Yes… probably. Of course.

But that's not the question.

MOTHER: What other question is there?

DAUGHTER: What was I thinking?

MOTHER: When?

DAUGHTER: Getting pregnant. Having a baby. When the world's so fucked.

MOTHER: Oh yes.

DAUGHTER: But I didn't know if I would get another chance. To have a baby again. And there he was just growing inside me. I just had to do nothing and everything would change. So that's what I did. I just did nothing. I felt oddly calm about it. And then I felt like I wanted to come home. I just said 'yes'.

MOTHER: Of course you did. You did the right thing.

DAUGHTER: Did I? To bring a child into this world and not have another person to share them with?

Sometimes, when I'm holding him and it's the middle of the night and he won't sleep. I shout at him. I have shouted at him with this voice, this amazing voice, not like my own voice at all. It's huge and from deep deep down. Like a real monster. It scares me. And I feel. I imagine letting my arms do what that voice is doing and just throwing him at the wall, because I feel so desperate, so desperately tired and lost and dead actually. Lost and dead.

And I imagine walking out, shutting the door, leaving him there. Because I can't cope mum. I can't.

I need help. I can't do this on my own.

MOTHER: But you're not on your own. You're not.

DAUGHTER: I want my son.

DAUGHTER stumbles to the bedroom to check on SAM.

MOTHER craddles her breasts. DAUGHTER re-enters woozy and defeated.

DAUGHTER: God I feel sick.

MOTHER: Lie down.

They'll be here soon.

DAUGHTER comes back.

DAUGHTER: He's so beautiful when he's asleep. I didn't want to disturb him.

MOTHER: Yes.

DAUGHTER damps a flannel and starts to clean her face.

DAUGHTER: There must be something I can do to help. What can I do?

DAUGHTER gets down on the floor again and shuts her eyes.

MOTHER: Let me.

MOTHER presses the flannel to DAUGHTER's forehead.

MOTHER: This will help.

They are both in the doorway.

DAUGHTER: All I want to do is pick him up and hold him. But I can't. Because it's not going to make anything better is it. It will just wake him up and make him unhappy.

MOTHER: You're a good mother Ella.

DAUGHTER: You just don't know that.

MOTHER: You are as good a mother as it is possible to be. There's only so good you can be.

DAUGHTER: What do you mean?

MOTHER: It's hard. It's more than hard. It's impossible. But. I want you to know that I don't believe for one moment that you would ever hurt him.

DAUGHTER: What does it matter what you believe? I could.

MOTHER: But I don't believe you will.

DAUGHTER: Okay.

MOTHER: I know one thing. I am very proud of you.

He's going to make you very proud one day too. You'll see.

...

I left you. When you were little. Younger than Sam. You didn't know that did you?

DAUGHTER doesn't move.

DAUGHTER: No.

MOTHER: Your father. He'd lost his job. This is when we were still living in Newcastle. We were broke and I think in my own way I was trying to make him face up to things. He'd get up every day, get dressed like he was going to work. Didn't change his alarm or anything. Just kept up the same routine for months.

You were maybe about six months old.

I tried to talk to him. I said. "Can't you see how tired I am?"

You didn't sleep much at first.

Anyway. I said to him, "I need you to help. To get up in the night. To change some nappies every day. I can't go on like this, not without you pulling your weight, with no money coming in for any childcare, or someone to help with the cleaning." And he said, "Okay."

So I woke him up the next morning at 5 am. I woke him and gave him a bottle, all ready. All he had to do was give you the bottle and hold you, while I had something to eat and then maybe a bit of a sleep. But he said, "I get up at 8."

"That's when I get up." He said. I'll never forget it. And he was snoring again, in seconds.

So I kicked the bed and said, "Well your daughter is up now and I'm going out."

And I didn't come back for a week.

Didn't even kiss you goodbye. I was so angry.

I booked myself into a B&B around the corner and slept all day. The first day.

When I woke up I telephoned and do you know what?! He had his Mum and Dad round doing everything and telling him what a lazy bitch I was.

DAUGHTER: And you stayed together?

MOTHER: Well I did love him you know. And then they the oil was found, right here on my island. So I came home and he had a job for life. We settled down. We put the hard times behind us.

And then I said to him, years later. I said, "Did you miss me that week I went away?"

I mean we were never apart for more than a night or two after that, for the rest of his life. That's two decades we were together with just one week apart.

And do you know what. He said I was making it up. That I never left. That I'd read it somewhere, that it was something I had seen in a film or a play and that I'd just imagined it was me.

And I couldn't prove it.

I couldn't prove it at all.

What with his parents both having passed away

And do you know what really pisses me off.

DAUGHTER: No.

MOTHER: I don't know.

Maybe it didn't happen.

Maybe I just want it to be true. Maybe it was a fantasy. Because how could I have left you on your own with him, with you still breast feeding and only tiny. How could I have done that? I couldn't, could I?

I must have tricked myself into thinking that I did it.

DAUGHTER: The B&B would have a record.

MOTHER: It's not there anymore. It's just a house now, well flats actually. I checked.

DAUGHTER: Is that why you haven't been much help then?

MOTHER: What do you mean?

DAUGHTER: Is that why you haven't been much help with Sam? I came back here to have him because I thought you'd enjoy it. I thought it would make us closer. I wanted it to.

But you haven't. It hasn't.

MOTHER: I've been helping all the time!

DAUGHTER: When?

MOTHER: I come round nearly every day.

DAUGHTER: You come round when he's napping. You come round, keep me from going to bed and then you play with him after I've fed and changed him. You only have the nicest bits. You're no actual help. I have to look after you too. Listen to all your little worries and council gossip.

MOTHER: I bring food.

DAUGHTER: Half the time it's got meat in it.

MOTHER: I forget occasionally. It's not on purpose.

I cleaned your flat from top to bottom when you were in
the maternity hospital.

DAUGHTER: That's true. You did.

*DAUGHTER looks around at the bathroom floor, her hand with
dried blood on it and her mum.*

MOTHER sighs.

MOTHER: The thing is Ella.

I found a lump.

Here.

She puts her hand on her right breast.

DAUGHTER: Oh. I see.

MOTHER: I'm telling you. Because.

DAUGHTER: Because you've found a lump.

MOTHER: Yes.

DAUGHTER: When did you find it?

MOTHER: A while ago.

I'm not dying.

DAUGHTER: No. God. No. Of course you're not.

MOTHER: I'm young.

I'm going to be fine.

DAUGHTER: Yes. Yes. I'm sure you are.

What does the doctor say?

MOTHER: I'm having both the breasts removed.

Next week.

DAUGHTER: I see.

…

MOTHER: Can you come with me?

DAUGHTER: Yes. Yes. Of course.

…

I'm sorry.

MOTHER: Yes. Me too.

…

I'm so scared Ella.

DAUGHTER puts her hand carefully on MOTHER's arm.

DAUGHTER: It will be alright.

You'll see.

You'll be alright.

MOTHER: Do you think?

DAUGHTER: *(She checks her watch or the phone for time.)* Half
an hour and the sun will start rising. It's one of the few
benefits of being up all night. You find these hidden
moments in the day, like just now, the moment before the
day starts. It's the most…. It's the best part of the day.

MOTHER: I don't want to die.

DAUGHTER: I know.

Let's go to the beach and watch the sun come up.

MOTHER: We could.

DAUGHTER: I take him out now to feed him on the beach quite often and watch the day uncover.

MOTHER: You wrap up I hope!

DAUGHTER: Of course.

...

Did you know that every dawn is an apocalypse?

MOTHER: Is it a joke?

DAUGHTER: No. Well. No. But the word "apocalypse", we use it to mean death, devastation, "the end of things", but it actually means "to uncover"...to reveal.

It's sort of funny ...because it's usually when I feel the best I do all day!

We'll go to the beach together.

MOTHER: Okay. Yes. Why not.

DAUGHTER: ...

Did you really swallow that key?

MOTHER reaches inside her bra, brings out the key and gives it to DAUGHTER.

They smile.

THE END

By the same author

MONEY: The Gameshow
9781849435055

Crossings
(Published by Sgript Cymru)
9780954371067

WWW.OBERONBOOKS.COM

Follow us on Twitter @oberonbooks
& Facebook @OberonBooksLondon